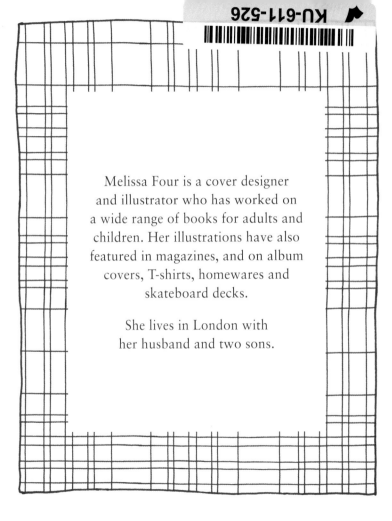

Melissa Four is a cover designer
and illustrator who has worked on
a wide range of books for adults and
children. Her illustrations have also
featured in magazines, and on album
covers, T-shirts, homewares and
skateboard decks.

She lives in London with
her husband and two sons.

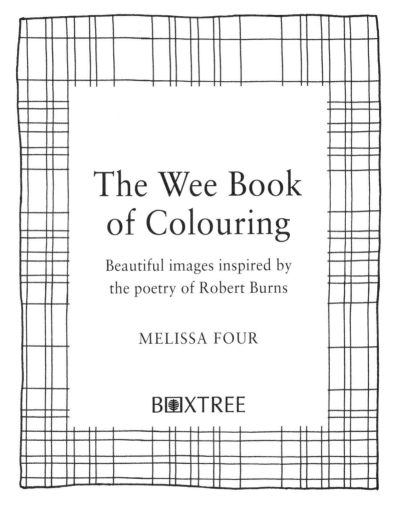

The Wee Book of Colouring

Beautiful images inspired by
the poetry of Robert Burns

MELISSA FOUR

BOXTREE

First published 2015 by Boxtree
an imprint of Pan Macmillan
20 New Wharf Road, London N1 9RR
Associated companies throughout the world
www.panmacmillan.com

ISBN 978-0-7522-6610-7

1 3 5 7 9 8 6 4 2

A CIP catalogue record for this book is available from the British Library.

Printed and bound by CPI Group (UK) Ltd, Croydon, CR0 4YY

Visit www.panmacmillan.com to read more about all our books and to buy them.
You will also find features, author interviews and news of any author events, and you
can sign up for e-newsletters so that you're always first to hear about our new releases.

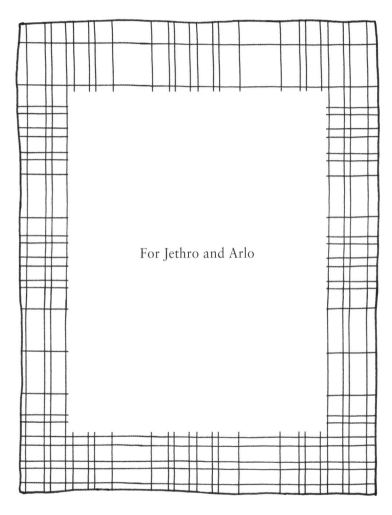

For Jethro and Arlo

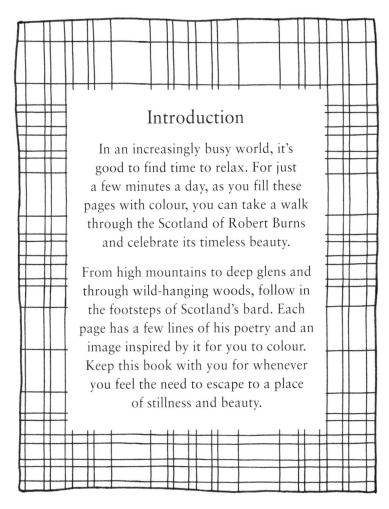

Introduction

In an increasingly busy world, it's good to find time to relax. For just a few minutes a day, as you fill these pages with colour, you can take a walk through the Scotland of Robert Burns and celebrate its timeless beauty.

From high mountains to deep glens and through wild-hanging woods, follow in the footsteps of Scotland's bard. Each page has a few lines of his poetry and an image inspired by it for you to colour. Keep this book with you for whenever you feel the need to escape to a place of stillness and beauty.

Wee, sleekit, cow'rin, tim'rous beastie,
O, what a panic's in thy breastie!

'To a Mouse'

As fair art thou, my bonnie lass,
So deep in luve am I:
And I will luve thee still, my dear,
Till a' the seas gang dry.

'A Red, Red Rose'

My heart's in the Highlands, my heart is not here;
My heart's in the Highlands, a-chasing the deer;
Chasing the wild-deer, and following the roe,
My heart's in the Highlands, wherever I go.

'MY HEART'S IN THE HIGHLANDS'

Flow gently, sweet Afton, among thy green braes,
Flow gently, sweet river, the theme of my lays;
My Mary's asleep by thy murmuring stream,
Flow gently, sweet Afton, disturb not her dream.

'SWEET AFTON'

The trout in yonder wimpling burn
That glides, a silver dart,
And safe beneath the shady thorn,
Defies the angler's art.

'Now Spring has Clad the Grove in Green'

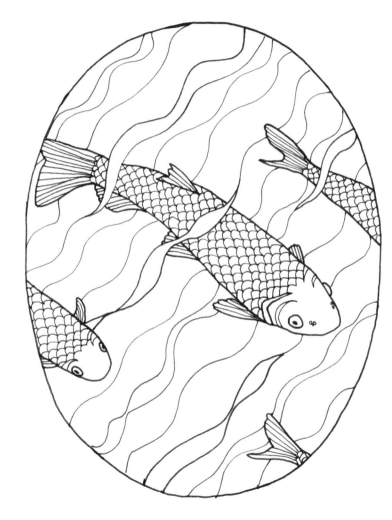

O my Luve's like a red, red rose
That's newly sprung in June;
O my Luve's like the melodie,
That's sweetly play'd in tune.

'A RED, RED ROSE'

Gin a body meet a body
Coming thro' the glen,
Gin a body kiss a body,
Need the warl' ken?

'COMIN' THRO' THE RYE'

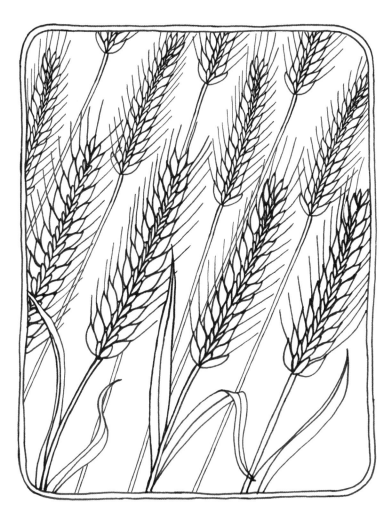

Sing on, sweet thrush, upon the leafless bough,
Sing on, sweet bird, I listen to thy strain,
See aged Winter, 'mid his surly reign,
At thy blythe carol, clears his furrowed brow.

'SONNET WRITTEN ON THE AUTHOR'S BIRTHDAY'

.

Now Simmer blinks on flow'ry braes,
And o'er the crystal streamlet plays,
Come, let us spend the lightsome days,
In the birks of Aberfeldie!

'BIRKS OF ABERFELDIE'

Fair fa' your honest, sonsie face,
Great chieftain o' the puddin-race!
Aboon them a' ye tak your place,
Painch, tripe, or thairm:
Weel are ye wordy o' a grace
As lang's my arm.

'ADDRESS TO A HAGGIS'

We twa hae paidl'd in the burn,
Frae morning sun till dine;
But seas between us braid hae roar'd
Sin' auld lang syne.

'AULD LANG SYNE'

The rough burr-thistle, spreading wide
Amang the bearded bear.

'EPISTLE TO MRS SCOTT'

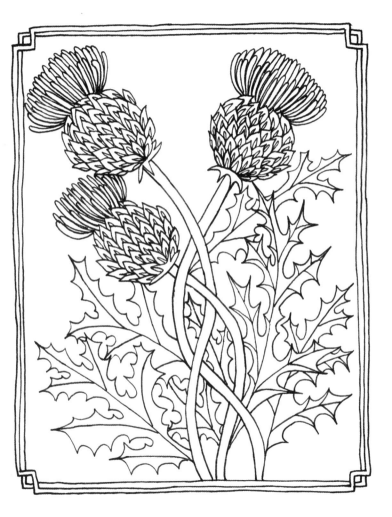

Let other poets raise a fracas
Bout vines, and wines, an' drucken Bacchus,
An' crabbit names an' stories wrack us,
An' grate our lug:
I sing the juice Scotch bear can mak us.

'Scotch Drink'

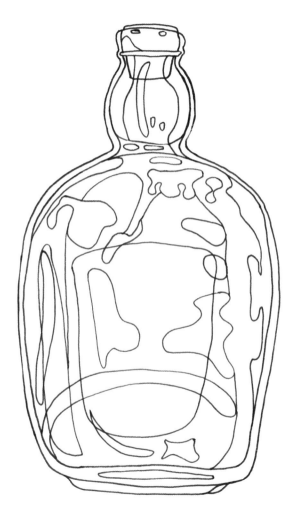

We think na on the lang Scots miles,
The mosses, waters, slaps and stiles,
That lie between us and our hame.

'Tam O'Shanter'

The wanton coot the water skims,
Among the reeds the ducklings cry,
The stately swan majestic swims.

'SONG COMPOSED IN SPRING'

How sweetly bloom'd the gay, green birk,
How rich the hawthorn's blossom;
As underneath their fragrant shade,
I clasp'd her to my bosom!

'HIGHLAND MARY'

Speaking silence, dumb confession,
Passion's birth, and infants' play,
Dove-like fondness, chaste concession,
Glowing dawn of future day.

'THE PARTING KISS'

Amang the trees, where humming bees,
At buds and flowers were hinging, O,
Auld Caledon drew out her drone,
And to her pipe was singing.

'A FIDDLER IN THE NORTH'

I ken't her heart was a' my ain;
I lov'd her most sincerely;
I kiss'd her owre and owre again,
Amang the rigs o' barley.

The sun he is sunk in the west,
All creatures retired to rest.

'IN THE CHARACTER OF A RUINED FARMER'

Upon that night, when fairies light
On Cassilis Downans dance,
Or owre the lays, in splendid blaze,
On sprightly coursers prance.

'HALLOWEEN'

Aft hae I rov'd by Bonie Doon,
To see the rose and woodbine twine:
And ilka bird sang o' its luve,
And fondly sae did I o' mine.

'THE BANKS O'DOON'

The birds sit chittering on the thorn,
A' day they fare but sparely;
And lang's the night frae e'en to morn,
I'm sure it's winter fairly.

'UP IN THE MORNING EARLY'

Oh, were yon hills and valleys mine,
Yon palace and yon gardens fine!
The world then the love should know
I bear my Highland Lassie, O.

'MY HIGHLAND LASSIE, O'

I dream'd I lay where flowers were springing
Gaily in the sunny beam;
List'ning to the wild birds singing,
By a falling crystal stream.

'I Dream'd I Lay'

Ayr, gurgling, kiss'd his pebbled shore,
O'erhung with wild-woods, thickening green;
The fragrant birch and hawthorn hoar,
Twin'd amorous round the raptur'd scene.

'To Mary in Heaven'

On a bank of flowers in a summer day
For summer lightly drest,
The youthful, blooming Nelly lay,
With love and sleep opprest.

The lav'rock in the morning she'll rise frae her nest,
And mount i' the air wi' the dew on her breast,
And wi' the merry ploughman she'll whistle and sing,
And at night she'll return to her nest back again.

'THE PLOUGHMAN'S LIFE'

O, were my love yon lilac fair
Wi' purple blossoms to the Spring,
And I a bird to shelter there,
When wearied on my little wing.

'O, Were My Love Yon Lilac Fair'

Rosy morn now lifts his eye,
Numbering ilka bud which Nature
Waters wi' the tears o' joy.
Now, to the streaming fountain.

'The Lover's Morning Salute to his Mistress'

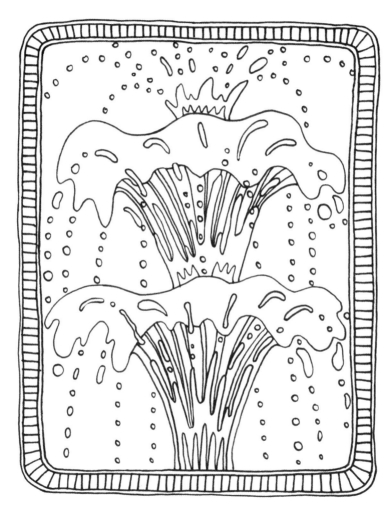

Wi' lightsome heart I pulled a rose,
Upon its thorny tree;
But my false luver stole my rose
And left the thorn wi' me.

'THE BANKS O' DOON'

The winter it is past, and the summer comes at last
And the small birds, they sing on ev'ry tree.

Among the heathy hills and ragged woods
The roaring Fyers pours his mossy floods;
Till full he dashes on the rocky mounds.

'Lines on the fall of Fyers Near Loch Ness'

There, in thy scanty mantle clad,
Thy snawie bosom sun-ward spread,
Thou lifts thy unassuming head
In humble guise.

'TO A MOUNTAIN DAISY'

Green, slender, leaf-clad holly-boughs
Were twisted, gracefu', round her brows.

'The Vision'

Then catch the moments as they fly,
And use them as ye ought, man!
Believe me, Happiness is shy,
And comes not ay when sought, man!

'A Bottle and Friend'

Farewell the glen sae bushy, O!
Farewell the plain sae rashy, O!
To other lands I now must go,
To sing my Highland lassie, O.

'My Highland Lassie, O'

But lately seen in gladsome green,
The woods rejoic'd the day,
Thro' gentle showers, the laughing flowers
In double pride were gay.

'THE WINTER OF LIFE'

Yonder Cluden's silent towers,
Where, at moonshine's midnight hours,
O'er the dewy-bending flowers,
Fairies dance sae cheery.

'CA' THE YOWES TO THE KNOWES'

Farewell to the mountains, high-cover'd with snow,
Farewell to the straths and green vallies below;
Farewell to the forests and wild-hanging woods,
Farewell to the torrents and loud-pouring floods.

Now blooms the lily by the bank,
The primrose down the brae;
The hawthorn's budding in the glen,
And milk-white is the slae.

'Lament of Mary, Queen of Scots,
On the Approach of Spring'

The sun lies clasped in amber cloud
Half hidden in the sea,
And o'er the sands the flowing tide
Comes racing merrilee.

One night as I did wander,
When corn begins to shoot,
I sat me down to ponder
Upon an auld tree root.

'ONE NIGHT AS I DID WANDER'

I see her in the dewy flowers,
I see her sweet and fair:
I hear her in the tunefu' birds,
I hear her charm the air.

'OF A' THE AIRTS THE WIND CAN BLAW'

How pleasant the banks of the clear winding
    Devon,
With green spreading bushes and flow'rs
    blooming fair!

'THE BANKS OF THE DEVON'

A rose-bud by my early walk,
Adown a corn-enclosed bawk,
Sae gently bent its thorny stalk,
All on a dewy morning.

'A ROSE-BUD BY MY EARLY WALK'

The flowery Spring leads sunny Summer,
The yellow Autumn presses near;
Then in his turn comes gloomy Winter,
Till smiling Spring again appear.

'MY BONIE BELL'

O, fresh is the rose in the gay, dewy morning,
And sweet is the lily, at evening close;
But in the fair presence o' lovely young Jessie,
Unseen is the lily, unheeded the rose.

'LOVELY YOUNG JESSIE'